Ramblings

Helen Aitchison

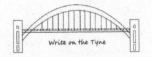

Published by Write on the Tyne

Ramblings

Helen Aitchison

Published by White...

Printed and bound in Great Britain by Clays Ltd, Elcograf S.p.A.

Paperback ISBN: 978-1-7394882-3-9
Cover design by Write on the Tyne
Cover image: www.pixabay.com

Published by Write on the Tyne
www.writeonthetyne.com

To Elise – the brightest star in my universe.

Albatross

Lingering,

In the shadows you lurk.

Although there have been a thousand sunrises,

Since I escaped from your claws.

The desire to feel truly emancipated,

Care free.

No looking over my shoulder.

No heart racing,

Dry mouth anxiety.

Albatross,

I crave to be without you.

To drown you in a sea of no regret.

To witness you fly away,

Never to return.

Blow up a balloon.

Place you inside,

Watch you float,

Away.

Bury you in the sands of a foreign beach.

As hope embeds a seed in my mind.

Time passes,

Fear relinquished,

Strength feeds,

Flourishing.

Nourishing my soul,

I'm ten feet tall.

Soaring,

Smiling,

Silently strong.

Albatross, you retreat, shrink and starve.

Darkness will never conquer light.

Relief,

My senses devour the sensation.

When you return,

I'll remember,

I

Can

Win.

Alive

Butter kiss flowers,

Reflecting summer sunshine,

Make me feel alive.

A Reminder

I must remember,

To hold you and memorise your touch.

To listen to your soothing heartbeat,

As I rest my head on your chest.

To embrace your scent,

The softness of your skin.

To hold you,

Inhale you.

To etch into my mind the map of your skin,

The perfect imperfections of scars and freckles.

A reminder,

To remember you,

And your body,

For the day I can no longer touch you.

Autumn

Morning breaks, sunshine golden,
The birdsong plays in the sky.
Its own orchestra, audible amplification,
Undisturbed, if only for a while.

The aromatic flavours of autumn,
Linger subtly in the air.
Dressing gown and slipper time,
Sun freckles faded from our skin.

Garden flowers strain and wilt,
Sun heat, palliatively weak.
Wind turns sharper, rapidly cooling,
Nature taunting, creeping in.

Tree leaves transforming colours,
Caramel, honey, ruby rich red.
Lipstick shades of the woman we want to be,

Or the one we desire to kiss.

No bare-sleeved humans on the street,

Cosy knits, warming skin.

Adapting to the elements,

Caressing like a tender touch.

Contemplating autumn coats and gloves,

Only discovering half the pair.

Hands holding take-away coffees,

Sipping the satisfying liquid hug.

Autumn nights, soon to be winter,

Then spring and summer just as fast.

Grateful of shelter, comfort, and love,

Always a warm heart with you.

Awakening

Open your eyes,

Let them realise,

It was never lies.

Lucid summarise,

Doubt will capsize,

Loosen the ties.

The mind now wise,

Dismiss silent cries,

Through deep sighs.

To subsidise,

Your pained goodbyes,

With slow hi fives.

Absorbing night skies,

Coloured berry pies,

Blended in disguise.

Softly spoken reprise,

As the resistance dies,

Screaming compromise.

Life to scrutinise,

No void to demoralise,

Just joy to maximise.

Because of You

Love isn't the grand gestures,

The look at me,

Showy moments.

It's the little things,

That add up,

To make a big impact.

It's the way you kiss my head,

Each morning,

As I remain cosy in bed.

It's the gratitude for your packed lunch,

That always tastes better,

With the added ingredients of love.

It's the hand squeeze on the sofa,

As we sip a cup of tea,

Made to my perfect colour.

Love is gratitude for you,

For safety, never having,
To walk on eggshells.

It's consistency,
It's comfort,
It's home.
A place that exists because of you.

Birdsong

The birdsong,

Tells me you love me.

Leaves fall,

Tender kisses on my shoulders.

As night descends,

You envelop me,

I feel you far from sight.

Bloom

Let your roots keep you grounded and bold.

Let your branches remain strong,

When the wind attacks your core.

Let your leaves possess the tenacity,

To hold on through the harsh times.

Bloom,

Grow,

Flourish,

And nourish those around you,

With all your nurturing brilliance.

Breaking the Pattern

When your feet hurt,

Walk in the direction of rest.

When you're running in circles,

Alter the path.

When the first move is always yours,

Step back and wait.

When you forever catch, but fall alone,

Stop offering to cradle.

Expectation doesn't make others change.

Stop watering dead plants.

British Summer

Raindrops quenching leaves,

Dancing on the window frame,

Summer shower bliss.

Cuppa

A warmth in my hands, a sigh of contentment,
I'm mesmerised by your sight.
A gentle blow to cool, my senses soaring,
Holding on, clasping tight.

Will I dip a biscuit or two?
A digestive, a bourbon, a ginger snap?
Maybe half the packet will get consumed,
As the saucer rests on my lap.

Your caramel colour, just the right shade,
Milked to the perfect degree.
A hug in a mug, the answer to all,
Heaven in a cup to me.

Fancy a cuppa? Time for a brew.
Shall I put the kettle on?
Always a good time, for a cup of tea,

Night through to early morn.

One of life's pleasures, to show you care,

A hot, soothing liquid gold.

Makes a bad day better, a morning brighter,

A warm cuddle in the cold.

My favourite thing, an everyday must,

A delicious cup of tea.

How do you take it? I'd love to know.

No sugar, just milk for me!

Desire

Tenderly touching,

Giggling beauty.

Lip-biting anticipation,

Tantalising tasting.

Innocently acting,

Intensely staring.

Wanting, not caring,

This moment, present.

Eyes undressing,

Heat radiating.

Heart accelerating,

Nervous combustion.

Mouths intertwining,

Oxygen starvation.

Butterflies in flight,

Fingertips electrical.

Insatiable hunger,

Skin magnetism.

Kiss me forever,

Melt into my being.

Elise

The baby that forever will be,

Even when you're forty years old.

The one and only,

Except for the cats,

Your shorter-term sisters.

You brought with you a connection,

Forever bonding us,

Over a love like no other.

An innocence,

that doesn't last long these days,

But your preciousness will eternally remain.

Our baby - my baby, if not by birth,

By heart.

The closest thing I would get,

To a love so unique.

You're brighter than all the stars in the universe,

More beautiful than any sunset in the world.

You're the most mesmerising of paintings,

And hold charm,

That if bottled and gifted,

Would make the world a better place.

And the world is a better place,

For having you in it.

Enough

I was always enough,

But your exponential greed,

Devoured my zest with no mercy.

Right place,

Wrong time.

Wrong look,

Right smile.

Exasperated from my soul.

A giggle of nerves.

A bundle of fear.

A screaming, adrenaline heartbeat.

A cry of lost hope,

Carried away in the wind.

As the thunder of hatred rumbles.

I was always enough.

But your exponential greed,

Devoured my zest with no mercy.

Eric

Forever a morning creature,

You rush to the opening door,

Desperate for affection,

Purring your greeting of love.

Chattering, tail curling around my leg,

Like a ribbon full of static.

As I stiffly bend to the ground,

Talking in a language you undoubtably understand.

Yawning, crispy-eyed,

Craving some of the morning persona you wear so

well.

You stretch, then bounce off your front paws,

Head touching my hand as I sit on the carpet,

Close to you, mountain and tree.

Kissing your apricot-coloured head,

Inhaling the fragrance of your fur,

As you purr like the engine,

Of the world's finest car.

Paw to my face,

Telling me you love me,

As you head butt my cheek.

And you do love me,

As I love you.

The cat-shaped hole in my heart,

Now filled.

Follow Me

Follow me to the sea,

Hear the waves caress my senses.

Follow me to the sea,

Where the sun shines on endless water.

Follow me to the sea,

Carry my weight in the infinite blue.

Follow me to the sea,

Where hate floats away to the horizon.

Follow me to the sea,

Let it wash pain and fear far away.

Follow me to the sea,

Where regret drowns in the vast current.

Follow me to the sea,

Sail our love on a boat made for two.

Ghost Town

I drove through town today.

Bustling bodies,

And tentative traffic.

The same old.

Yet different enough,

To feel like another life.

A world where familiarity was you,

At the bus stop,

On a Monday afternoon.

Taking me into shops,

That sold anything, everything,

You could want and don't need.

Long gone.

Demolished.

Repurposed.

Invisible at the bus stop.

Only there in my mind,

Smiling with your bingo win.

Yet still I slow down.

Searching for you,

Amongst a queue of strangers,

In my town,

My own ghost town.

Hands Around my Heart

Your hands held me after birth,

Mother's mother with skills to share.

But a different relationship,

Precious gem in the jewelled eye.

You held my hand as I grew,

Yours decorated with age spots,

And a thick, gold wedding ring.

Embraced me through the years,

I was never too old for cuddles.

Until you became too aged to hold tight,

And I'd wrap my arms around you,

Your softness, your love,

Still radiating through me,

Like the most comforting cup of tea.

Your hands, elderly, soft and pale.

Crepe paper creases, thin skin.

Always elegant.

Beautiful, nails painted.

Fragility correlating with increasing years.

My love grew deeper,

Rooted in a history,

That I wish was longer,

But would never be long enough.

You held my hand all my life,

I held yours as you died.

Thin silk slipping through my fingers,

Dissolving the hope of recovery.

The touch impossible to forget.

I hold it in my mind,

Like I held those hands - tight, with love.

Now the ageing hands are mine,

And they remind me,

Every now and then,

Of yours.

Minus the irreplaceable love.

Haunted

You haunt me,

And I don't know,

If I need it,

Or hate it.

The discomfort,

The memories,

Grabbed at.

Worried one day,

They'll evaporate.

Anxious that pain,

Is the only way,

To remember,

I love you.

As the words,

Are no longer said,

No longer heard.

Just an echo,

In an empty space.

Your reassuring touch,

Fading as the days pass,

Faster than my heart can repair.

You're there,

Unrequested,

At times when I can't process.

Caught out,

Winded,

Wounded,

By the air snatching punch,

Of your vacuum.

You haunt me,

And I don't know.

If I need it,

Or hate it.

Heavy Load

Inside the serpent,

You crawl and you creep,

Like poison flowing,

Through my veins.

Darken my soul,

Seep through my pores,

Clamber out in droplets,

Of sweat.

Leave a stain on my bed,

A bad taste in my mouth,

A scar on my flesh,

Never healing.

Creep away in the night,

Insidious toxicity,

Search for the soul of another,

To pollute.

Crucifying presence,

Blanket of cold discomfort,

Heavy,

Heavy,

Heavy,

The weight that accompanies you.

A burden.

The world on my shoulders,

Is what they say.

But we can grow stronger,

The weary strain, alleviated.

Carrying our oppressive load,

Until it becomes lighter, dissolves.

We flourish with our strength,

We'll be okay,

I promise.

Hello and Goodbye

Hiya,

Hello,

How do you do?

Welcoming greetings to share.

Alright,

Howdy,

Morning,

A conversation to show you care.

Bye-bye,

Good night,

So long,

A wave of the hand as you go.

See you later,

Alligator,

In a while

Crocodile,

A goodbye to make you chuckle so.

A hug with a hello,

Goodbye and an embrace,

Even greeting strangers,

Produces smiles on their face.

So talk to people, old and new,

Pass the greetings on.

A smile and kindness brightens days,

And helps us all to get along.

Holding On

Grab my hand, my darling,

Pull me into our new beginning.

Where your love fuels my courage,

And your belief makes me certain,

That everything will always work out.

Encase your hand in mine, my love,

Fingers slotting into each other,

Like they were made to be a pair.

No words, my dear,

Just your gentle smile,

Caressing my soul.

Grateful for your endless devotion.

Anywhere with you,

Is everywhere I want to be.

Home

A tender kiss on my head,

You inhale the shampoo fragrance.

Arms embrace me protectively,

Warming my coldest days.

I realise home isn't a place,

With walls, windows, and doors.

Home is a simply a feeling.

The feeling of home is you.

In Sleep

In my dreams I can reach you,

Hold you.

You feel like the person I remember.

When you were you,

And not a disintegrating shell,

Out of reach.

When our time was just ours,

And your love was mine.

I wake,

You're gone,

But I still feel the warmth of your presence.

In The Shadows

There, in the corner of my eye,

Telling me you're still here.

Ebbing and flowing, weak and strong,

Never going far, always near.

I see your shadow, sense your coldness,

Certain you have your own smell.

How much is my imagination?

I can never truly tell.

'You've been expecting me,' you say,

With your poisonous laugh and sneer.

It's true, I accept that now,

Your sinister power I don't fear.

History repeating, your forever act,

This is your perfect performance.

Your insistent presence, your leading role,
Your creeping, jubilant dance.

Ardently stalking the vulnerable,
You forever prey on the weak.
Targets, you identify and inflict,
Many too fearful to speak.

No discrimination in your method,
Your insidious Russian roulette.
Once you enter the personal realm,
You've secured your winning bet.

So many of those before me,
Countless more on the list.
I feel you taint the atmosphere,
Your dark shadow in the mist.

Your shift is never over,
Working around the clock.

Once acknowledged, the fear is real,

You taunt, you tease, you mock.

Until your victim succumbs,

You linger, watch and wait.

Never presenting yourself fully,

Until the sealing of the fate.

Until your cruel crescendo,

The reason why you came.

To take another soul away,

Death, Death is your name.

Light the Sky

Darling,

Catch the stars in the sky.

Use them,

As our nightlight.

Let them lead us,

On our path,

To happy ever after.

Little Pat

Your eyes bright,

Like the midnight stars.

Your toothless smile,

Could melt the coldest of hearts.

Kissing your tiny head,

Covered in a forest of fluffy hair.

I inhale your scent,

You smell of innocence,

Of love,

Of hope.

If only we could bottle it,

And share it with the world.

Love Is

If love is a look,

It's a smile as you glance my way.

If love is a feeling,

It's my soul's contentment.

If love is a touch,

It's your safe enfold.

If love is a sound,

It's your comforting voice.

If love is a place,

It's here in your arms.

If love is a person,

My person is you.

Memories of the Heart

Your face in a photograph,

A memory,

A fragment of time captured.

Inked on my mind,

Painted on my heart,

Forever, your image of eternal love.

As time passes,

Weeks turn to months,

The space between us evades me.

But in a moment of silent calmness,

The touch of your hand,

Feels like only yesterday.

Meow Off

Screaming cats warning,

Hissing, big tails, and arched backs,

Marking territory.

Mindful

Wishing time away,

Please be summer,

I can't wait until...

As ironically I want,

The day with you to last forever.

Inhaling sensations,

While I crave more,

Of something, anything.

Be in the present, absorb,

Let our spirits escalate,

Like a cheer at a football match.

Stop wishing life away.

Grip my hand,

Kiss my cheek.

Silent, focus,

Etch this memory in our minds for eternity.

When you wish for the future,

For time not present,

Recall this memory,

This place,

Us.

Remember this consuming feeling,

Sensation of love,

Of togetherness,

Of completeness.

Remember this memory of us.

Mistakes Made

Do I sit by your grave and weep,

A heart too broken for love to keep,

A mind to tired for restful sleep.

Do I search in the sky above,

To the answer of forever lasting love,

The wedding-freed turtle dove.

Do I stare at your name on a list,

Thinking of times our lips kissed,

As loneliness swallows me, sombre mist.

Do I freeze time as I stare,

Empty space, no longer a pair,

The world moving on without care.

Do I let the inner voice scream,

For the moments lost and could have been,

As I stand alone, the erased team.

Does your image colours fade,

Like the memories we made,

And endless mistakes made.

Do I sit by your grave and weep,

A heart too broken for love to keep,

A mind to tired for restful sleep.

Moments

Kiss me at midnight,

Hold my face to the moon.

Look into my eyes,

Moments pass too soon.

Take a snapshot of memory,

Engrained on the brain,

The stars in the night sky,

The earth smell of rain.

Touch your fingers with mine,

Interlocked, connected soul.

No need to speak words,

Comfort, a shared goal.

Dissolve in my smile,

It lights the night sky.

A beacon of happiness,

Between you and I.

No one else in this world,

Our own space and time.

Alone on this planet, I'm yours, you are mine.

Never Far Away

I'm the sun caressing your face on a summer's day.
I'm the whistling wind as you hold your collar tight.
I'm the birdsong melody echoing through the sky.
I'm the feeling of deja-vu trapped in your mind.

I'm the blooming spring flowers, colouring your world.
I'm the patch of snow that never seems to melt.
I'm your skipping heartbeat felt once in a while.
I'm the familiar scent that makes you smile.

I'm the reflection erased in a second glance.
I'm the feather falling at your patient feet.
I'm the coincidence one too many, that never was.
I'm the scar etched forever on your heart to carry.

Never far away.

Our World

Walk with me,

Forever we will be,

As one in the moonlit sky.

An adventure to find,

Love, one of a kind,

Your hand resting in mine.

A tender embrace,

Our own private space,

I feel like we own the world.

A love to behold,

Stories yet to be told,

Our first chapter starting now.

Part of the Family

Love isn't only reserved for humans.

There is a special place in our hearts,

That can be occupied by an animal,

A paw print on our heart.

From rescue to forever home,

Finding one another.

Part of the family,

As if always meant to be.

Offering unconditional thanks for a chance,

In life, a home, kindness.

Gratitude shown through a knowing love,

Affection when we often need it most.

Loyalty, companionship, a connection.

Understanding that just being there,

Can sometimes be the ultimate help.

Years pass, months turn to remaining days,

Our four-legged family members leave.

The rainbow bridge crossed,

Paw print stamped forever on our heart.

As their food bowl remains empty,

And their blanket cold,

Encasing their faint fragrance.

Precious memories to comfort us,

As we never forget the love,

Gifted to us by our family pet,

That no human could ever provide.

Patience

Hold the weight of my worries,

Throw them up in the sky,

Watch them crash with a thud to the ground.

As my heart beat pounds,

Like a drum in the desert,

Never making an audible sound.

Let the wave wash over me,

In out, no change,

Just the fragrance of hate on my face.

As the words whirl and scream,

Without meaning a thing,

No solace to be found in this place.

Don't stay with me, go,

Run away, never return,

They'll trap you, force you to stay.

A prison of locked hope,

Enslaved dreams and belief,

Escape, run quick, keep away.

Is this my forever dark truth?

Or a movie,

On repeat each new day.

Dulled by more tablets,

To smoother my mind,

Controlling me in every way.

My brain stripped of thought,

Am I me anymore?

Or just a shadow of all my past.

A big, bold performance,

The audience does wait,

To see the role that has been cast.

Hear me, listen closely,

Understand I'm no harm,

As I battle conflict in my head.

I am the same old me,

Fighting against the storm,

To smoother fear, darkness and dread.

A new day will come,

A future to have,

This isn't how I'll always feel.

Have patience with me,

Support and soothe,

So my mind can recover and heal.

Pause

In the crisp autumn leaves,

We walk, peaceful silence,

No need to talk.

You place your hand,

Gratefully in mine.

That moment,

Just us.

Paused in time,

Together entwined.

Peach

Hand wrinkles, forming slowly.

The first cracks in the arid earth.

They look like yours;

Pale,

Gentle,

Kind.

But never the velvety softness,

That encased your slender hands,

As if silk was your skin.

Your wedding band,

Still moulded onto your frail finger,

Like it was the only one the world created.

Sat, proud,

Still shiny,

Radiant with love.

That was lost decades ago,

But still felt with every exhale.

Silently staring at my palms,

Turning them slowly,

Eyes shut,

Hoping they open to yours.

Those hands that cherished us all,

And wiped away a million tears.

Ageing skin,

Ageing memories,

But with a void that never feels old.

As I look at my pale hands,

And wish they were holding yours.

Pocket Watch

Your pocket watch ticks with my heart.

The beat of love with time.

The now,

The future,

The yearning for the past.

To go back, turn back time.

To tell you again,

You were everything.

Your love soaked me,

Nurtured me,

Made me feel protected.

You were everything,

And my gratitude still beats in my heart,

That ticks with your pocket watch.

Possibility

Love is a place that only we know,

A space where you are always my echo.

Where the warmth of your heart,

Is hotter than the sun,

Permeating my soul to glow,

With a happiness only you offer.

It isn't words,

Not even actions.

But a feeling.

As if the blood in my veins is you.

In sync,

Effortlessly connected,

Our harmonious unity.

And I realise,

Nothing is impossible,

When you're by my side.

Precious Jewels

Summer kissing,

Dream chasing,

Days that never end.

Carefree laughter,

Of innocence,

Melody filling the air.

Absorbed, imprinted,

Inscribed in the mind.

Memories forever held,

Like a locked treasure chest,

At the bottom of the ocean.

Our precious jewels,

Part of our tapestry,

That cost nothing,

But are priceless.

Presence

Cold hands,

Warm soul,

Rough skin,

Smooth role.

Fluid being,

Rigid mind,

Harsh ways,

Gentle kind.

Frozen smile,

Urgent shove,

Hello goodbye,

Fast love.

Quick kiss,

Slow hand,

Long gaze,

Strong stand.

Reasons Why

Tick

Tock

Move or stop.

Fight

Flight

Freeze or flop.

Run

Hide

Seek them out.

Lightening

Strikes

Scream and shout.

Name

Called

Turn around.

Knock

Ring

Make no sound.

Key

Turn

Run away.

Plead

Beg

Retreat, stay.

Yes

No

Decision time.

Him

Her

Yours or mine.

Life

Death

Take a chance.

Fly

Free

Killers dance.

Safe

Peace

Hope and pray.

Leave

Rebuild

There is a way.

Reassurance

Wipe the tears from my eyes, honey,

Push the hair back from my face.

Touch me,

Reassuring warmth,

Fuel this desolate space.

Encompass me, darling,

Lift my face to the sky.

Tell me the stars shine with hope,

That they shine for you and I.

Reflection

The mirror on the wall, I stare hard at the face,
Once a child, now an old woman, here in life's race.
All the images I've seen, etched on my brain,
Thoughts in my head, could make me insane.

Every mark, every wrinkle, reflected to my eye.,
Those I wanted to disappear, God, I did try.
The lotions the potions, the make-up used,
Covering, hiding black eyes, skin bruised.

Shame and deceit, the windows to my soul,
A black charred heart, that once was whole.
It all boldly stares back, forty years of hate,
Can my smile be real, or is it too late?

Will my eyes glow, with the curling of my mouth?
Does my face light up, as my cheeks head south?

Can happiness greet me, at this time of life?

Does may face wear well, all my trouble and strife?

As I put on the lipstick, the powder and blush,

Dare I feel happy, as my heartbeat does rush.

I don't look half bad, for an old bird they say,

My face tells a story, I did it my way.

Onwards and upwards, I know it's true,

I see behind me, the reflection of you.

You smile in the mirror, a kiss on my skin,

My blackened heart changing, warmth from within.

Can this broken woman heal? You think so,

You won't walk away, you won't turn and go.

Love can enter our lives, anytime, anywhere

Your reflection is real, I know that you care.

Risk Taker

Chasing adrenaline,

Into the night.

You duck and dive,

You love and fight.

Broken and fixed,

The catch on the gate.

Too soon, just on time,

Or painfully late.

The fix, the buzz,

The injection of desire.

Every thought consumed,

Don't extinguish that fire.

An itch, a scratch,

That won't go away,

A game with the devil,

You must now play.

Shell Collector

I've collected people like shells on the beach,

As I've walked my journey across the sand.

A magnificent collection of diverse shells,

All colours, sizes and conditions.

Some older, with a crack, a scar,

But still they remain strong,

Defiant to the elements of life.

Many less shiny but never dull,

Waiting with resilience for the sea or sun,

To polish them,

Nurture them,

Heal them.

They all glisten.

They all glow.

Beautiful in their place, their purpose, their

presence.

And I'm grateful for every single one I collect,

Who equally collect me and connect me.

Shining

Can't take my light from me,
Snatch it away leaving dark.
Dull my shine with your shadow,
Can't suppress my spark.

Won't let the wind drag me down,
Whip my feet up from the ground.
Can't let it take my breath away,
Absorb my voice, my sound.

The rain won't drown me of belief,
Can't submerge my dreams of tomorrow.
Water will flow but not carry me away,
Instead, hope will triumph over sorrow.

Sun will prevail, the joy of beginnings,
Growth, strength, blossoming soul.
Elements beaten, conquered and won,
Acceptance as my being feels whole.

Shop Strangers

I saw you in the shop today,

I wondered what your story told.

Of your life, your love, your loss,

As I smiled behind a mask.

Watching you push your trolley,

Purchasing food for one.

I longed to know what happened,

To the person that made you two.

I hoped you hold the memories tight,

The snapshots of love in your mind.

From times gone by, of better days,

Forever present in your heart.

I saw you in the shop today,

I wondered what your story told.

Of your life, your love, your loss,

As I smiled behind a mask.

Some Days

Some days you are,
Everywhere.
In the whistle of the wind,
In the reflection of puddles.
In the warmth of the sun,
Your scent in the air.
Some days you are,
Everywhere,
In each direction I glance,
Yet never in my view.
In the beat of my heart,
In the tears that cascade.
Some days you are,
Everywhere,
In the music that's played,
In the memories of old.
In routines and habits,
Present, there with me.

Sparkle

Leave a little light in the world,

A glimmer of hope.

A crack in the darkness,

A beacon of faith.

That the sun will shine for you,

And your dreams may just come true,

The day will bring a new,

Way to show you,

You are loved.

Speechless

No words needed,

As we sit side by side.

Hearts interlinked,

Hands intertwined,

It's only us on this planet.

Spoons

I, fit perfectly with you.

Spoons.

Me the cold one,

You, hot,

Like you've been stirring tea.

I, fit perfectly with you.

The missing jigsaw piece,

That evokes a smile of completeness.

I, fit perfectly with you.

Hand to glove,

Protecting me from the elements.

I, fit perfectly with you.

The Awareness of Self!

For all the things I'm rubbish at,

There is another side.

Where I'm brilliant and capable,

Completely bonafide.

I may not know my left from right,

Or how to read a map.

How to use iCloud,

Or fix a leaking tap.

Instructions often baffle me,

remembering passwords, it's a no.

Giving directions, not a strength,

But I'll give anything a go.

None of us are perfect,

We all have limits within.

But for each and every struggle,

There's a goal we'll always win.

So focus on the positive,

You can only do your best.

Find a friend around you,

To help with all the rest!

The End

Did you find the place you were looking for,

The seat that was shaped just for you?

The meaning of life, well yours, at least,

Did the lies begin to come true?

Did the person you needed recruit you,

Like a soldier, going to war?

Did you sense salvation, adventure, and chance,

Behind the guarded door?

Did you have your eureka moment,

When at last, it all made sense?

Did you fit the pieces together,

Dissolving the need for pretence?

Did your happy ever after appear,

Like a puff of smoke fairy tale?

Was success found in round two,

Of what with me, resulted in fail?

Did you find new year, new you,

As poisonous layers melted away?

When the truth of your warped reflection

Prevented me wanting to stay.

Did you discover a new identity,

Hidden amongst the rot?

A hope, transformation, a free pass,

For redemption, your only shot.

There, Forever Within

Silence, in a vacuum,

Yet I can hear all the things,

You don't say.

Coldness, in a tepid room,

Lingering, chilling the air,

Like crisp winter.

Punch in the stomach,

The wind taken,

Out of my sail.

Lost words, I can't remember,

Conversations I crave,

To hear you, once again.

Memories battle in my brain,

To never be forgotten,

Turn to debris.

I smell you in the air,

For a moment, reality alters,

You're here with me.

Reminders of you,

Never to heal.

But my heart still beats,

With your permanent tattoo,

There, forever within.

The Unwritten Rule

There's an unwritten rule between the best of
friends,

That shit happens,

And we can't always be one hundred percent.

But affinity isn't measured on a scale.

The rhetoric of friendship,

Subjective to the drawing of our own circle,

That we sometimes skim the edges of.

We flow,

We slow,

We fall,

We stop.

Friendship,

There in the forefront or background,

With strength of the eye-squinting, summer sun,

Or the cool breeze when less paramount.

But always there,

Our weather of friendship.

The celebrations and commiserations,

The victories and voids,

The prosecco and the plaster,

The magic and medicine,

Depending on that critical phone call,

The one that we've all had.

Friendship,

No distance or time,

Can dissolve the superglue of history,

No matter how far it dates back,

Or how busy lives are.

Demands, family, work,

And the time-stealing routine,

That is simply life!

Friendship,

A constant in a volatile world,

Uninterrupted, perpetual solidarity.

The unwritten rule between the best of friends.

The Warmth of You

Days pass in a heartbeat,

Except when sadness descends.

My days are extended and tormented,

Like the tortured soul I feel.

In that frozen moment,

Cold loneliness,

Where the blank wall,

Returns no answer,

Regardless of my removable gaze.

You arrive, the day feels brighter,

Lifted by your nourishing smile,

That permeates my skin.

Like the Californian rays,

Your laughter, the warmest blanket,

On the coldest of empty nights.

As your presence makes time pass,

In a heartbeat once more.

The Women We Are

My world is full of the women I could have been,

And I don't mean the singer, actress, or model.

I mean the girl begging on the street,

For her next, desperate fix,

Or for her lads' next hit,

That will stop the hit to her face,

For a few hours at least.

My world is full of the women I could have been.

The woman running, hiding,

Always looking over her shoulder.

The woman who lives out of a suitcase,

Who knows every train line like her bank pin code.

The woman who never makes friends,

As she's never there long enough,

And the door of trust is boarded up,

Alongside the houses she's fled.

My world is full of women I could have been.

The woman selling sex from the damp flat,

In the "rough" part of town.

With the mouldy windowsill and book thin mattress,

That holds stories of trauma and delight,

Depending on who you listen to.

My world is full of women I could have been.

The care leaver residing courtesy of His Majesty's

Pleasure,

For attacking the man who took her bright

innocence,

And turned it forever dark.

My world,

Your world,

Our world.

Women we are,

Women we've been,

Women we could be.

Today

I thought of you,

Today,

As I instinctively itched my upper arm.

The soft, loose skin,

Against my fingers,

Where muscle tone and youth fade.

I thought of you,

My smile spread,

As quick as the tears fell.

And I remembered,

How I used to wobble the flesh on your upper arms,

And we would laugh.

Those arms that held me,

Comforted me.

The arms that even when I held you instead,

Still felt like pure love.

I thought of you,

Today.

Together Is My Favourite Place

Take my hand, walk across the sand,

Don't turn and look behind.

As I whistle in your ear, the song I can hear,

Whilst the waves crash on the shore.

Feel the wind on your skin, the warmth within,

A squeeze of your hand in mine.

All the nights in the dark, until I ignited that spark,

Will never be undone.

The twinkle in your eye, a star in my sky,

Together is my favourite place.

So take my hand, walk across the sand,

Don't turn and look behind.

Treasure

Hold me in my dreams,

As I sleep.

Your touch,

A treasure I can find.

Where your pain-free smile,

Radiates the room,

And your laughter plays on repeat in my mind.

Uncomfortably Illuminated

I breathe, underwater.

And sometimes, I can't see,

Through the dark daylight,

That surrounds me.

Obstacles,

In my way.

A heavy load,

Carried each day,

To a destination unknown.

As I guess and predict,

Sometimes I get it right,

Switching on the light,

Uncomfortably illuminated.

Like watching the world,

Through a snow-globe shake.

Hazy,

Cloudy,

Foggy-camera take.

Yet still I strive,

Juggle and try,

As I breathe, underwater.

Wear Your Skin

Wear your skin,

Embrace each lump,

Respect each bump,

They tell your tale.

Wear your skin,

Let it breathe,

And slowly weave,

The story of you.

Wear your skin,

Say, 'It's all mine,'

Let your beauty shine,

From inside out.

Wear your skin,

Each imperfection,

Your intricate connection,

To the person within.

Wear your skin,

Accept the being,

Love what you're seeing,

No change needed.

Wear your skin,

Let your reflection smile,

Self-love may take a while,

Let it begin!

Weight Loss

I lost the weight,

Of other people's opinions,

That have nothing to do with me.

Of the worry about things I can't change,

Can't control,

That drip from a tap I can't turn off.

Of rumination that's toxic,

Stamps on joy and creates anxiety.

Of views that are none of my business.

I lost the weight,

Of my past that's gone,

Stagnant, buried.

Not able to alter,

Only forward I can move.

Lighter, freer, absorb the positive,

Change, opportunity, and love,

Without the weight of negativity.

I lost the weight,

Never to be found.

Wilted Herbs

Hearing not listening,

We see with no reflection.

Wanting, not needing,

As we let our dreams die.

Like the herbs on our windowsill,

Wilting.

Or expect to fly,

Propelled by another.

Reaching not grabbing,

Scrambling,

As our dreams die.

Winter Love

Ice cold park hello's,

Hugging our coats as we walk.

My hand, warmed by love.

Yellow Roses

Another minute, day, week since you went,
Another second in the past of the time we last
spent.
No more voice or smiles, just those on a screen,
No chance to explain the importance you mean.

As the images of you stay engrained in my mind,
The void runs deep, but strength I must find.
No holding your hand, softness of your skin,
No gentle embraces, your warmth from within.

Can't share the stories that made you laugh,
Excited to see you as I dash up your path.
No, 'Hello, it's just me,' calls on the phone,
No, 'Watch what you're doing driving home.'

A sense, a smell, a sound or a touch,
Desperate connection when I need it so much.

Not here, nor there, yet forever in the room,

Never ready for loss, always too soon.

Flowers in the window, memory fragrant in the air,

Etched on my heart, in the skin that I wear.

Around me so vividly, but hidden from sight,

I hold you there in my soul, day and night.

Acknowledgements

Thank you for buying this poetry book - filled with the ramblings of my mind, that sometimes present themselves in the middle of the night, or make me pull over when I'm driving to jot down thoughts!

My writing journey began with poetry and my first published pieces were two poems for an anthology supporting mental health charities.

I wasn't a fan of poetry at school and being told who and what I should read and like. But I'm a big fan of words, meanings, emotions, and connections - and that's all that poetry is. My favourite poets are people who feel real to me and who leave me reflecting. I hope Ramblings has had this impact on you.

Massive thanks for reading my book and please take a minute to review it on Amazon and Goodreads, which help make books visible to other readers. Reviews also attract more book sales, which is very important for Ramblings as all proceeds go to Age UK North Tyneside. I am lucky enough to be on the board of trustees of this incredible charity, which supports people aged over fifty in our community.

Profits from Ramblings will help the phenomenon team to deliver critical and preventative services and allow older people to enjoy life in a way age should never dissolve.

Thank you to everyone who's inspired my poetry and all the life situations, good and bad that have made me learn and develop. Thank you to my partner, Paul, who not only inspired many of these musings, but also helps with the often complicated process of creating the end product. Paul, you will always be my favourite story.

To find out more about my writing and Write on the Tyne (CIC) please visit:

www.helenaitchisonwrites.com
www.writeonthetyne.com

Social media links are also available through the websites.

Age UK North Tyneside was established in 1972 and has grown to become the largest local voluntary organisation in the borough. They have over 300 staff and over 70 volunteers providing a wide range of services for older people in North Tyneside.

Age UK North Tyneside services include:
- Free and confidential information and advice
- Specialist dementia support
- Fitness classes and social groups
- Support for veterans
- Older LGBTQ+ support
- Help at home
- Will writing

And much more...

To find out how they can support you or your loved ones, call 0191 280 8484 or visit ageuk.org.uk/northtyneside.